IF YOU DON'T BRUSH YOUR TEETH

written by EDWARD JAZZ   illustrated by MARÍA FLÓ

Dedicated to my kids, who helped create this book, and are great at brushing and flossing! – EJ

To my parents, without whom, I wouldn't have such a beautiful smile. – MF

ISBN: 978-1-7373255-0-5 (Paperback)

ISBN: 978-1-7373255-1-2 (Hardcover)

Visit us online at www.kidsbooksrule.com

Once there was a little girl who wouldn't get ready for bed.

"Time to brush your teeth!" her mother called.

"Nope," said Remi.

"If you don't brush your teeth, I'll read
one less book tonight," said Mom.

"If you read one less book, I'll put your **shoes** on the roof," said Remi.

"If you put my shoes up there, you can't watch TV all week," said Mom.

"If I can't watch TV, I'll bury the **remote control** and **tortillas** in the garden," said Remi.

"You'll miss your favorite shows."

"No dessert for you tomorrow!" said Mom.

"If I can't have dessert, I'll cover your bed with **raspberry jam**," said Remi.

"If you cover my bed with jam, you will have to sit in timeout for ten minutes," said Mom.

"After timeout, I'll put the dog and cat in a **hot air balloon**," said Remi.

"Then I will send you straight to bed," said Mom.

"No way," said Remi. "I'll take my
little brother and move to Mars."

"When you return home, you will have to clean out the cat's litter box," said Mom.

"Ewww! Gross!" said Remi. "If I have to clean it out,
I'll put frogs and pancakes in your gym bag."

"If you do that, you will have to clean all
the dirty dishes tomorrow," said Mom.

"I'll sing 'Peanut Butter Toot Toot Eating Up the Fruit Fruit' forever," said Remi.

"If you sing that song, you can't play
board games all week," said Mom.

"Instead, I'll fill your pillow with
ladybugs and **broccoli**," said Remi.

"Then you will have to take out the trash," said Mom.

"If I have to take out the trash, I'll put your sunglasses and rain boots in the *washing machine*," said Remi.

"If you do that, you'll have to vacuum
the whole house," said Mom.

"If I have to vacuum, I'll take all the CUPS and mail them to Grandpa," said Remi.

"In that case, you can't have a play date with your friends tomorrow," said Mom.

"If I can't have a play date, I'll put fifty-six holes in the wall and fill them with *tofu*," said Remi.

Mom took a deep breath and looked down at Remi.

"Then I'll fill your room with one thousand rabbits and lock the door." Mom smiled.

Then she looked up and asked,
"Wait. Would they **POOP** in there?"

"Yes," said Mom.

"ok. I'll brush my teeth," said Remi.

Special Invitation...

Be the first to receive updates from Kids Books Rule!,
including free giveaways, new release announcements,
behind-the-scenes goodies, and much more!

Visit the secret link below to join:

www.kidsbooksrule.com/brush

We also make music!

We make educational (and sometimes silly!) music for kids.
Find Kids Songs Rule! everywhere you listen online.

www.kidssongsrule.com

A Note From the Author:

Thank you so much for your support. Every time you purchase from an independent author, someone is celebrating on the other end (me)!

If you loved this book, the sweetest thing you can do (even sweeter than raspberry jam) is to leave a review so that other readers will take a chance on Remi and her Mom.

Don't feel you have to write a book report. A brief comment like, "Can't wait to read the next book in this series!" will help potential readers make their choice. It really does make a difference.

★ ★ ★ ★ ★

www.kidsbooksrule.com/review

★ ★ ★ ★ ★

Thank you kindly, and don't forget to brush your teeth!

Edward Jazz

Printed in Great Britain
by Amazon

17885995R00022